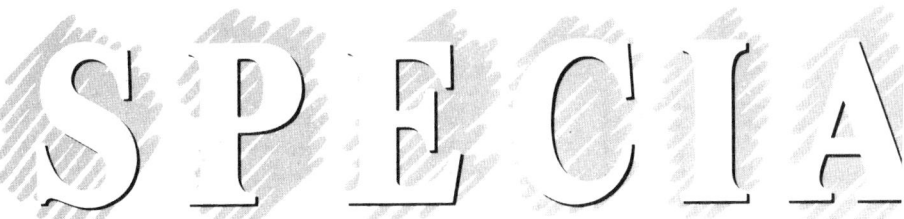

Science: The Living World

ALAN JONES
ROY PURNELL

Folens COPYMASTER

CONTENTS

Introduction	3-4
LIVING THINGS	
Notes and suggestions	5
The variety of life 1, 2 and 3	6-8
Environments	9
Habitats	10
Seasons	11
Pondlife	12
Air and living things	13
All living things	14
Farming seasons	15
Where there's muck ...	16
Nitrogen roundabouts 1 and 2	17-18
Food chains	19
OUR BODIES	
Notes and suggestions	20
Skin and touch	21
Taking care of your skin	22
Smoking can damage your health	23
Taste	24
Reactions	25
Your eyes	26
Animal eyes	27
Ears and hearing	28
All senses	29
Fooling your senses	30
Mirror tricks!	31
How good is your sense of touch? 1 and 2	32-33
Energy foods	34
Foods for health	35
Health farm	36
Teeth	37
Skeletons and organs	38
OUR WORLD	
Notes and suggestions	39
The world	40
Weather	41
Weather chart	42
Rain measuring	43
Make an air thermometer	44
Waste monitor	45
Natural resources	46
Rocks	47
Space	48

Acknowledgements

Nottingham Trent University, Clifton Lane, Nottingham NG11 8NS.
Gwent College of Higher Education, Caerleon, Newport, Gwent NP6 1XJ.

Folens books are protected by international copyright laws. All rights reserved. The copyright of all materials in this book, except where otherwise stated, remains the property of the publisher and author(s). No part of this publication may be reproduced, stored in a retrieval system, or transmitted, in any form or by any means, for whatever purpose, without the written permission of Folens Limited.

Folens do allow photocopying of selected pages of this publication for educational use, providing that this use is within the confines of the purchasing institution. You may make as many copies as you require for classroom use of the pages so marked.

This resource may be used in a variety of ways; however, it is not intended that teachers or students should write directly into the book itself.

© 1992 Folens Limited, on behalf of the authors.

First published 1992 by Folens Limited, Albert House,
Apex Business Centre, Boscombe Road, Dunstable LU5 4RL, England.

ISBN 1 85276291-8

Illustrations by Barrie Richardson and Ian Foulis Associates.

Printed in Great Britain by Ashford Colour Press.

SPECIALS! SCIENCE

The purpose of this text is not to try to convince the reader of the value of Science for all pupils, as this has now become an entitlement of the modern curriculum. It aims to give some valuable, practical learning opportunities for all pupils but mainly for pupils who experience specific learning difficulties.

Science can be a great motivator for all pupils, including those who often experience failure and suffer low self esteem. It has been recognised that suitable experiments, investigations or relevant problem-solving activities can be great motivators. They can give enjoyment and a willingness to work at a task producing a sense of success, as there are no 'right' answers when solving a suitably chosen problem. A solution can be as valid as anyone else's, providing it solves the problem. All solutions have value and with discussion and some help can lead to the pupils reaching an even higher level of achievement. Science-based activities can help pupils to realise that even a 'wrong' answer is a valuable experience if you can explain why the answer was inaccurate, and it can help to produce a better solution next time. The greater the number of scientific activities, the better the pupils become in using the skills acquired.

Special Needs: what does it mean?

Research has shown that the proportion of pupils with special educational needs can be as high as 20% of the school population. These pupils need either permanently or on a temporary basis, some form of help to overcome their barrier to learning.

Learning is a very individualistic process and what works for one person does not necessarily work for another. It is probable that every pupil has a problem with some aspect of their education at some time during their school life, but the pupils under discussion here have a problem most, if not all, of the time. The barriers to learning are general and applicable to a wide range of pupils, some have particularly well developed intellects, whereas others have limited academic ability, but all have some abilities that must be used, valued and exploited.

The practical activities in this book will try to open up areas of science to all pupils who can benefit from it.

Our philosophy is that ability rules over disability.

PROBLEM AREAS	SUGGESTED SOLUTIONS
Language difficulties, both received and communicated, might be confused; pupils can have word fixations.	Use simplified language and many simple diagrams, drawings or pictures, videos and frequent teacher/helper contact.
Children can be slow to see connections between things e.g., causes and their effects or doing experiments and seeing the relevance of the results; poor at making intellectual or knowledge links.	Use small step-by-step instructions and easily understood concepts, together with a close contact with a teacher to monitor progress.
Poor memory of situations and putting events into a logical or working sequence.	Help pupils by not using systems that are dependent upon memory and give clear instructions to help sequencing of events.
Unable to work effectively on their own due to a lack of personal confidence; they need teacher support to help structure their life and work patterns.	Give constant support and help and put pupils in a group of supportive pupils; science activities are often best tackled in groups.
Often passive in class; do not ask questions or see the need to ask questions.	Develop motivating activities and make them colourful, noisy, smelly, or make it so that the pupils will want to show someone their results, or do further activities.

These learning barriers may be accompanied, in some cases, by pupils showing immaturity in social and emotional development.

PROBLEM AREAS	SUGGESTED SOLUTIONS
Impulsive behaviour; inappropriate reactions to new social or school situations; cannot see how their own behaviour affects the attitude of other people; little restraint of anti-social behaviour.	Choose safe, secure, familiar activities; keep the pupils active with achievable step-by-step work on motivating experiments to prevent time for frustration.
Cannot easily make friends with peer group, but might be more at ease with adults or younger children.	Choose activities that can be supported by the teacher as well as the members of the peer group.
Egocentric/selfish behaviour; inappropriate play toys; selfish habits and interests for their age.	Choose interesting experiments with a chance to communicate results to others in words or drawings; if possible match activities to their areas of interest and hopefully extend these to a more suitable level.
Can be socially isolated or alternatively can be seekers of attention or affection.	Value the contribution and quality of work by the pupils and express this openly to the pupils and the class at the appropriate time.
Cannot easily detect (or are insensitive to) the 'body language' or non-verbal communication of others.	Select suitable activities and pupil classroom groupings with a chance to communicate results to others. Give an important task to the person to help them communicate.

For some pupils the barriers might be those of physical disabilities or sense impairments but many pupils also have associated cognitive problems e.g., their spatial awareness, or not being able to apply simple concepts to new situations.

PROBLEM AREAS	SUGGESTED SOLUTIONS
Can have difficulty in interpreting two and three dimensional diagrams, maps, pictures, graphs etc.	Use the most appropriate method backed up by a multi sensory set of information, verbal, diagrams, tactile, actual apparatus to touch and use. Everyone has a preferred mode. Care must be given to the best way of doing worksheets and diagrams.
Can have difficulty in drawing to scale and drawing things in perspective.	Use actual apparatus together with diagrams and relate apparatus sizes in diagrams to objects they know and can appreciate the actual size of.
Can have difficulty in processing information in one mode, e.g. verbal, and then putting the instructions into action or in diagrammatic form.	Use a multi sensory and multi media set of instructions.
Pupils with physical disabilities might need slight modifications to apparatus and equipment.	Some pre-lesson planning can either find an equivalent alternative or produce a solution to the physical problem by using an adaptation.

Not all the pupils will have all these characteristics and it might be that you recognise items *you* have difficulty with! There are barriers to learning in some cases brought about by a physical or sensory disability. However, a disability does not automatically mean that there is a gross learning barrier. It is therefore important not to hinder a pupil learning by hanging a label around their neck, e.g., that of 'blind', MLD, SLD, Spina Bifida etc. as some people often assume the label automatically means inability to think or do practical tasks. That is not the case, as there are as many variations of *degree* of disability as there are *levels* of abilities. It is best to look at the *abilities* of the pupil rather than putting stress on the pupil's *disabilities*.

Living things - notes and suggestions

The variety of life (Sc2: 4a, 5a, 5f, 5g)
The questions are intended for discussion as well as written response and they can be changed and adapted for your own pupils. Pupils might look at the picture and the teacher can verbally ask the questions one at a time or put the questions on a sound tape for the pupils to use at their own pace.

Environments (Sc2: 4b, 4a)
This introduces the concept of living things suited to life in different environments. The distinction between a habitat - a place to live - and an environment - the conditions at that place - is one that pupils often have difficulty with.

Habitats (Sc2: 5a)
This gives a focus on the specific types of place that different living things have adapted to or prefer to live in. It is not usually successful to 'transplant' a set of living things from one habitat to another. A visit to a zoo, botanical garden, garden centre, butterfly farm, etc. could supplement this topic. Notice how humans live in a wide range of habitats. Why?

Seasons (Sc2: 4a, 5b)
The four pictures illustrate the situation in Britain where the seasons are distinct. Some countries do not have such a distinction. This is a useful discussion point. You could also discuss why some animals hibernate.

Pondlife (Sc2: 5f, 5g)
The examples given are the inhabitants of a typical British pond. Your local pond may contain a different community but the diagram serves to show the diversity of life that cannot be easily seen from the pond edge. A 'pond dipping' trip together with a classroom analysis of contents can be fascinating for pupils. Hand lenses or microscopes will be needed. A picture reference book of herbivores and carnivores could be helpful.

Air and living things (Sc2: 20)
The elephant loses a lot of heat energy through its large skin surface area but this is somewhat reduced by the thickness of the skin. The skin also prevents a lot of moisture loss and insulates from the strong sun.
Big animals need a lot of food. Do a survey of costs of food for the pupils' pets and compare costs with size of animal. The pupils could draw a diagram showing the food requirements of a mouse.
Fish can take the small amount of dissolved oxygen out of water. This is why indoor aquaria need to have air bubbling through them to keep up the amount of dissolved air. Human lungs are not able to cope with air dissolved in water.

Farming seasons (Sc2: 3a, 3b)
This shows the cycle farmers use to grow plants.

Where there's muck...
This scene can be acted out by the pupils. It helps them to sort out information from conversations.

Nitrogen roundabouts (Sc2: 3d)
The diagrams give scope for sequencing and provide good discussion points. Notice how air containing oxygen and nitrogen is essential to all living things (oxygen for energy release and nitrogen for growth). Pupils will need help to put them into the correct sequence.

Food chains (Sc2: 5c, 5d, 5e)
This activity encourages pupils to see links between living things in terms of prey and predator, herbivores and carnivores. When arrows are added to show the direction of food flow (eaten to eater), a more valuable food web will emerge. There is more than one food chain possible here e.g., worm > blackbird > hawk: plants > caterpillar > blackbird > hawk: plant > rabbit > fox.

NATIONAL CURRICULUM INFORMATION

The activities address science in the National Curriculum and can be cross-referenced to sections of the Programme of Study and topics mentioned in the Attainment Target level descriptions (levels 1–4). Some activities refer to more than one section and some to other subject areas.

The activities give opportunities for addressing Attainment Target 1, Experimental and Investigative Science, in a safe way.

The variety of life 1

Living Things — Your teacher will give you some questions about living things.
- Use this picture to help you answer the questions.

Living Things

The variety of life 2

1. Look for and colour the:
   poppy - red, dandelion - yellow,
   rose - pink, foxglove - purple.

2. What are the hedges for in this picture?

3. (a) List four different animals you can see.

   (b) List the 'wild' animals and 'domestic' ones.

wild	domestic

4. What animals could you expect to find in the house?

5. Where in the picture would you expect to find the following insects?
   (a) mosquitoes (b) honey bees
   (c) greenfly   (d) butterflies

   (a) _____ (b) _____
   (c) _____ (d) _____

6. Where in the picture would you expect to find most earthworms?

7. (a) Which animals in the picture live underground?

   (b) Why do they live there?

8. What are the people doing and why?

9. Where would the following living things live?
   (a) fox   (b) mole
   (c) goat   (d) field mouse
   (e) kingfisher (f) wild deer
   (g) spiders   (h) dog
   (i) grass snake (j) trout
   (k) badger   (l) chicken

   (a) _____ (b) _____
   (c) _____ (d) _____
   (e) _____ (f) _____
   (g) _____ (h) _____
   (i) _____ (j) _____
   (k) _____ (l) _____

© 1992 Folens Ltd.   This page may be photocopied for classroom use only   Page 7

The variety of life 3

Living Things

10. Describe how people have affected the countryside in the picture. Are any of those effects bad?

11. What do squirrels eat?

12. Where would you find the nests of:
    (a) skylark (b) blackbird

    (c) bluetit (d) house martin

    (a) _____ (b) _____

    (c) _____ (d) _____

13. Where will the frog lay its eggs?

14. What changes happen to frogs' eggs before they look like adult frogs?

15. (a) List the animals that give birth to babies that look like their parents.

    (b) Which of the living things lay eggs?

16. Name a tree that loses its leaves in the autumn.

17. Name a plant that lives in water.

18. Name a place where you would look for moss.

19. Which animals like to eat meat? We call these animals carnivores.

20. Write a story about a day out in the countryside.

© 1992 Folens Ltd.

Environments

Where animals and plants live their surroundings are called their ENVIRONMENT.

We talk about environments using words like cold mountains, dark forests. Can you see others in the picture below?

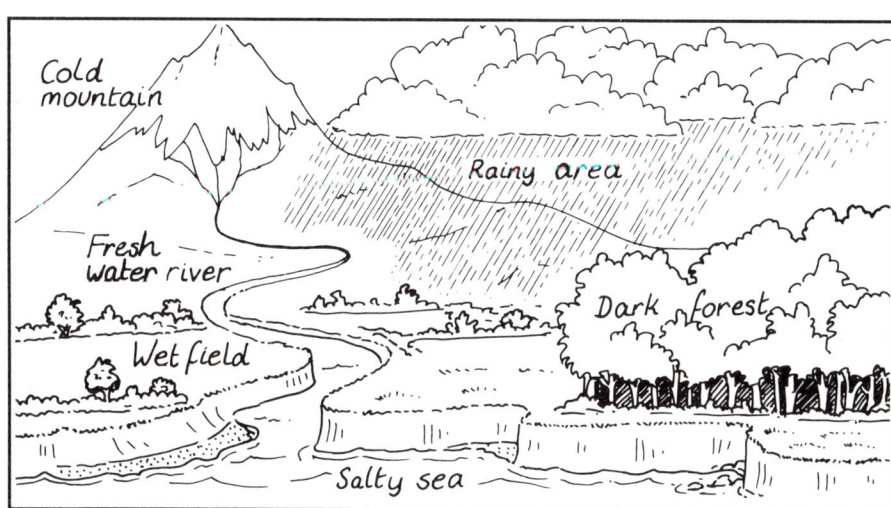

USEFUL WORDS
cold
dark
fresh water
wet
salty

- Fill in these environment words.

1. Sheep would live in the _____ field.

2. There might be birds in the _____ forest.

3. I might see trout in the _____ river.

4. Very few animals would like to live on the _____ mountain.

5. Animals such as seals usually live in the _____ sea.

Talk about why different animals live in different environments.

Habitats

Different animals and plants like to live in different places. This is called a habitat.

- Look at the pictures of six parts of the world.
- Choose animals and plants from these lists that you think live in each habitat.
- Fill in a table like the one below with the names you have chosen.

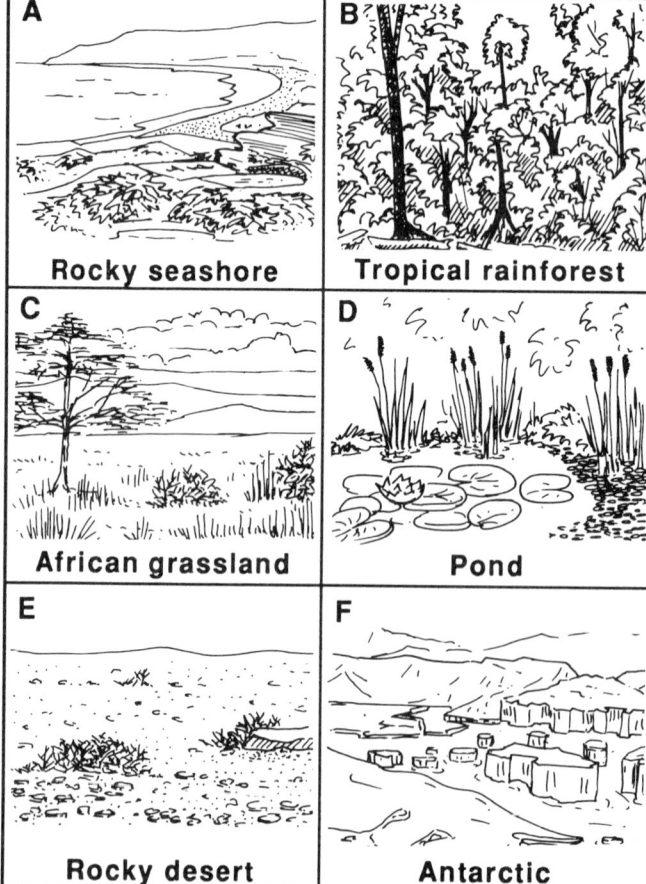

A Rocky seashore
B Tropical rainforest
C African grassland
D Pond
E Rocky desert
F Antarctic

ANIMALS
camel
crab
dragonfly
giraffe
gerbil
lion
monkey
penguin
shellfish
water flea
whale
zebra
humans

PLANTS
bulrush
cactus
duckweed
mahogany
seaweed
teak
water lily

Photo	Habitat	Plants that live there	Animals that live there
A	Rocky seashore		
B			

© 1992 Folens Ltd.   This page may be photocopied for classroom use only

Living Things

Seasons

Investigate

- Pictures A, B, C and D show the same habitat. Each picture shows one of the four seasons. Which picture goes with which season?

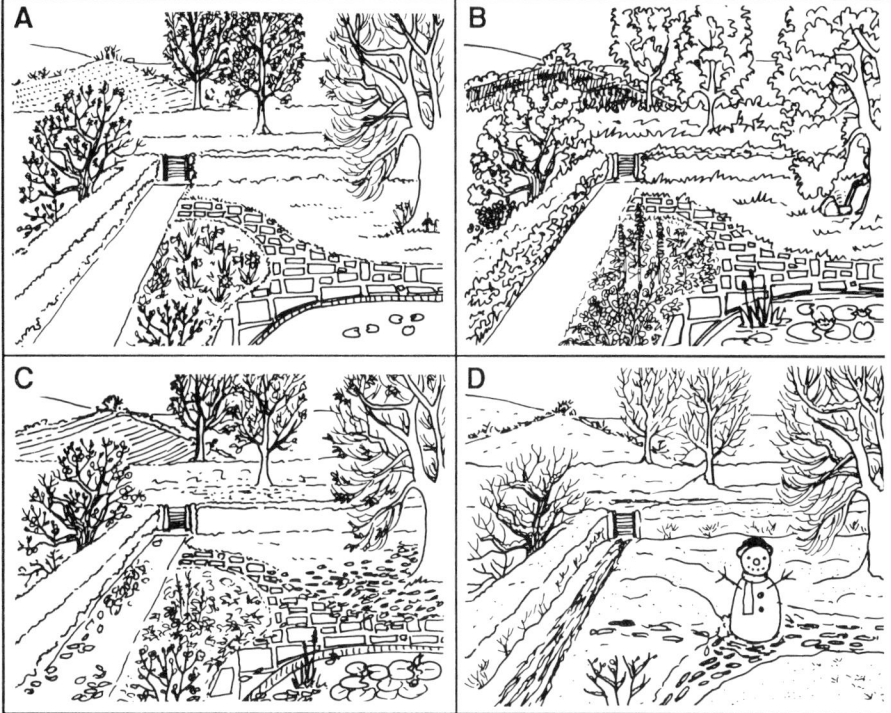

1. Name one animal that lives in this habitat all year around.

   _____

2. What food would that animal eat during each season?

   _____   _____

   _____   _____

3. (a) Name an animal that leaves the habitat during winter.

   _____

   (b) Why does it leave?

   _____

What I found

Talk about how humans have changed their habitat to help them survive extremes of weather.

© 1992 Folens Ltd.   This page may be photocopied for classroom use only   Page 11

Pondlife

Water is very important to all living things. Some things live in water all the time. It is their habitat.

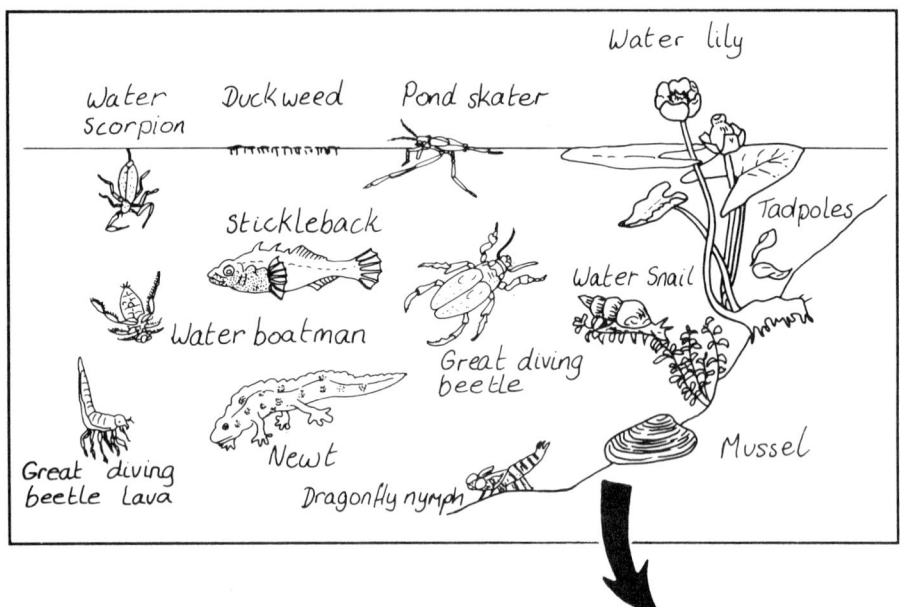

- Some plants live under water but their leaves float on the surface. Why?

  _____

  _____

- The animals that eat plants are called herbivores. The animals that eat meat (other creatures) are called carnivores.
- Name 2 animals of each type.

  herbivore 1 _____ _____

  herbivore 2 _____ _____

  carnivore 1 _____ _____

  carnivore 2 _____ _____

Talk about why there are more herbivores than carnivores.

Air and living things

All living things need air, water and energy to live. They get their energy from the food fuel they eat. Animals break down the food they eat in a special way to give energy:

FOOD + OXYGEN ⟶ WATER + CARBON DIOXIDE + ENERGY WASTE

- What sources of energy can you see in this picture?

  _____

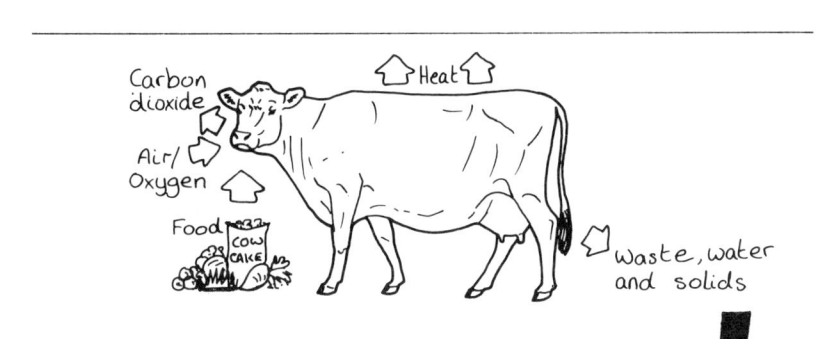

1. Draw a diagram to show **how** you use food to give energy.

2. How do underwater divers get the oxygen they need?

   _____

Talk about how fish get their energy.

Living Things

All living things

- Put a tick in the boxes below the living things if they need these to survive:

Needed to survive	animal	plant	humans
air			
sunlight			
water			
food			
reproduction			
soil			
a home			
friends			
transport			
music			

- All living things die at some time. What usually happens to the bodies of animals and plants after they die?

_____

Talk about what things make animals, including us, die.

© 1992 Folens Ltd.   This page may be photocopied for classroom use only   Page 14

Farming seasons

- Cut out these pictures and put them into the correct order to describe a year in the life of a farmer who grows plants.
- Stick the pictures into your book to show the farming cycle.

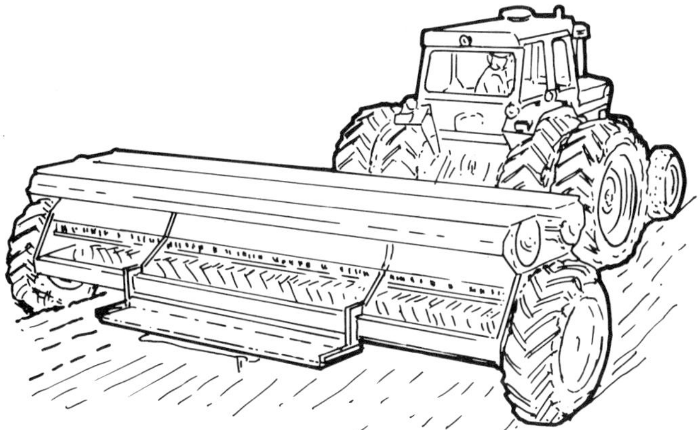

Sowing

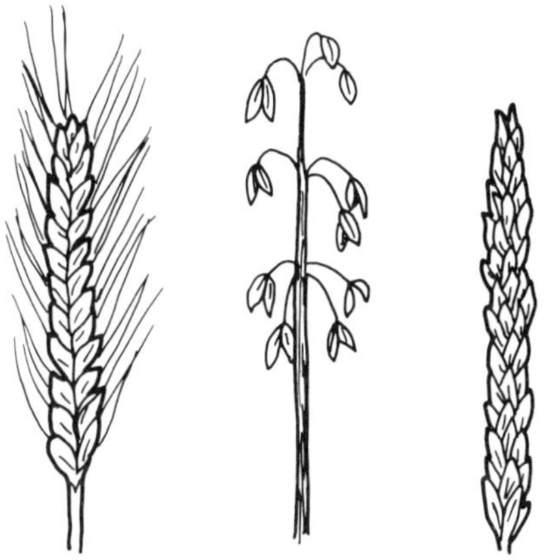

Fully grown cereal crops

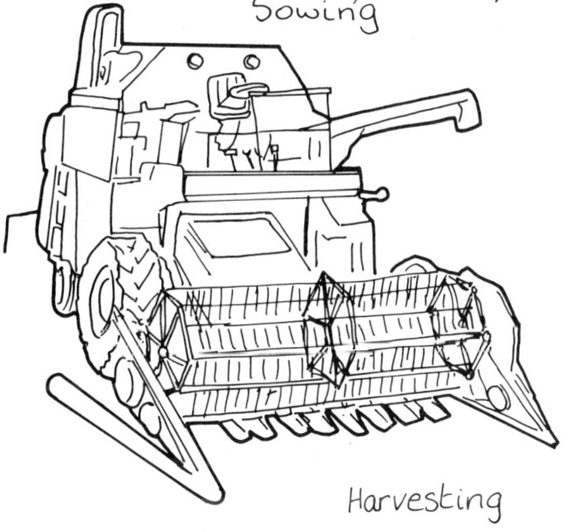

Harvesting

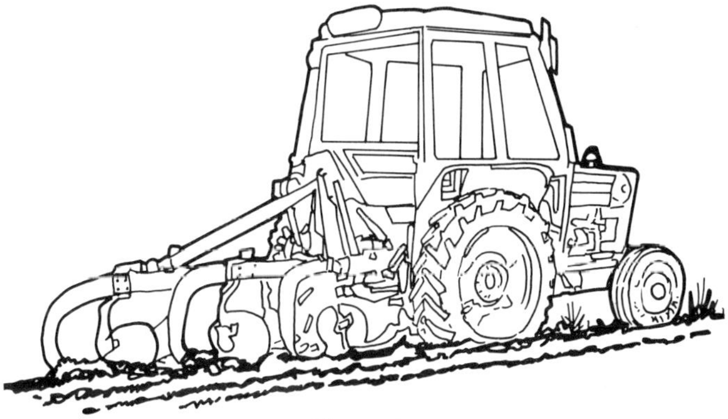

Ploughing

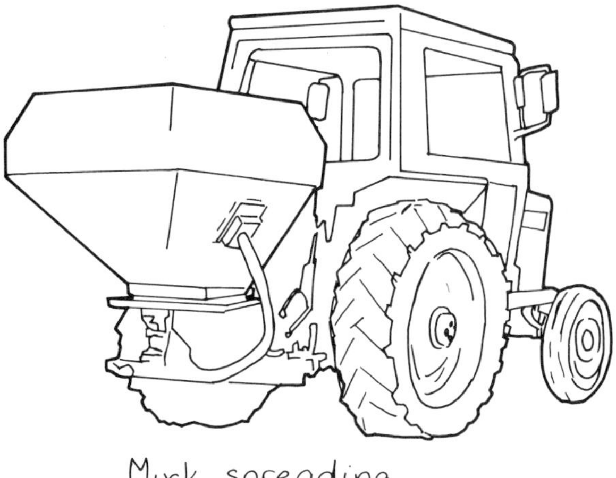

Muck spreading

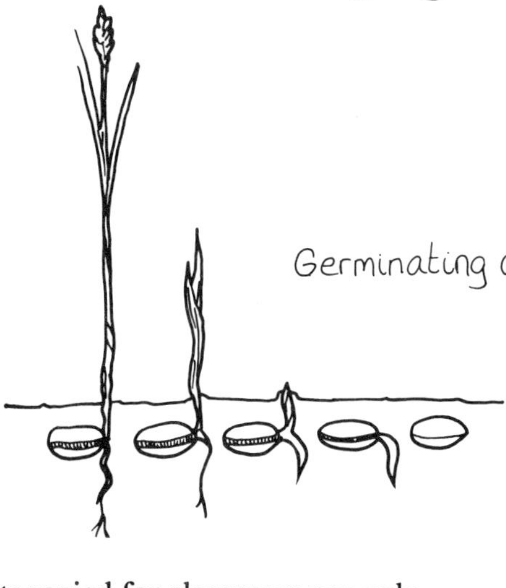

Germinating and growing

Where there's muck ...

- Read this story then make a list of what is needed to make a good compost heap.

Living Things

Investigate

Nitrogen roundabouts 1

Pictures A-J show where nitrogen comes from, how it is used by living things, and how it is returned to the soil and air again.

- Cut out and arrange your 'NITROGEN ROUNDABOUT' pictures on the sheet showing how the nitrogen goes from one place or living thing to another.
- Check your ideas with your teacher.
- If they are correct, paste them in your book and join them up by drawing arrows.

A. Plants with swellings on their roots use nitrogen from the air.

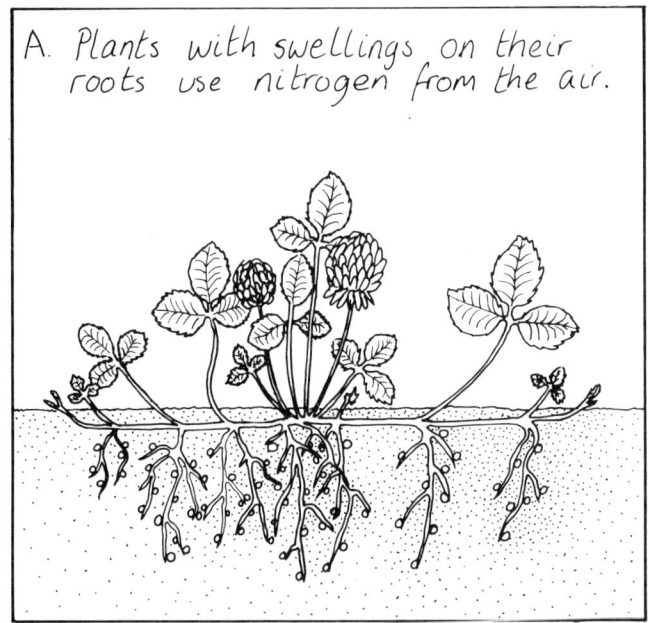

B. Animals die and decay.

C. Nitrogen is in the air.

D. Plants use nitrogen from the soil to grow.

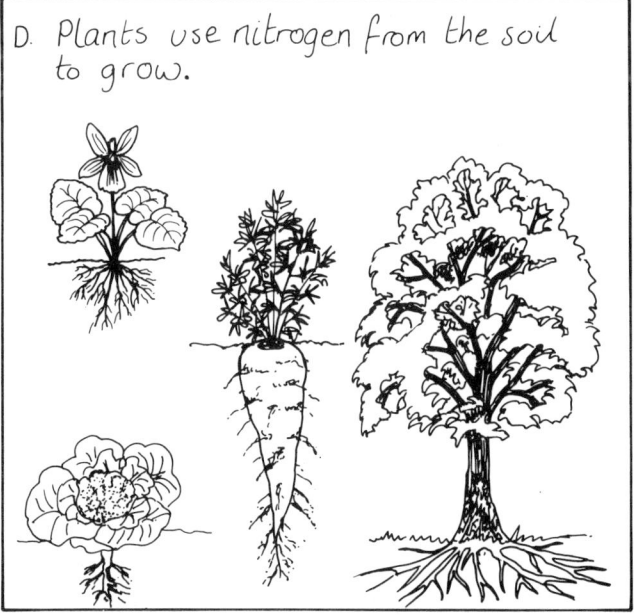

© 1992 Folens Ltd.   This page may be photocopied for classroom use only

Nitrogen roundabouts 2

E. Nitrogen compounds are in plants.
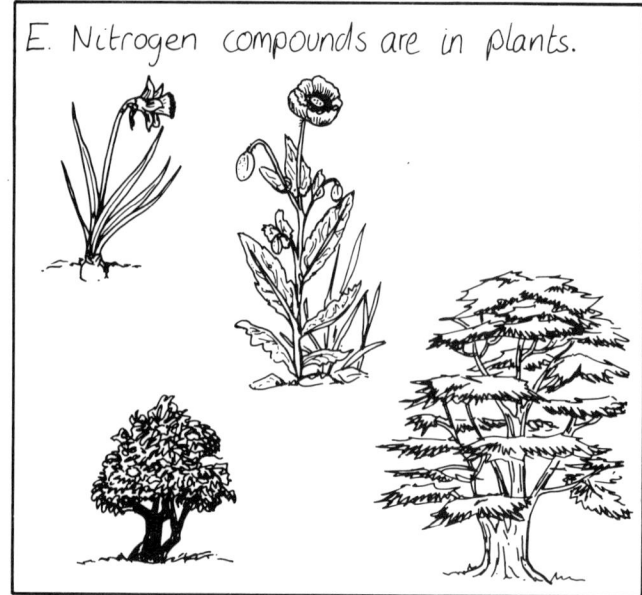

F. Plants decay.

G. Nitrogen chemicals are in animals.

H. Plants are eaten by animals.

I. Lightning makes simple compounds from nitrogen in the air. They dissolve in rain.

J. Nitrogen compounds are washed into the soil.
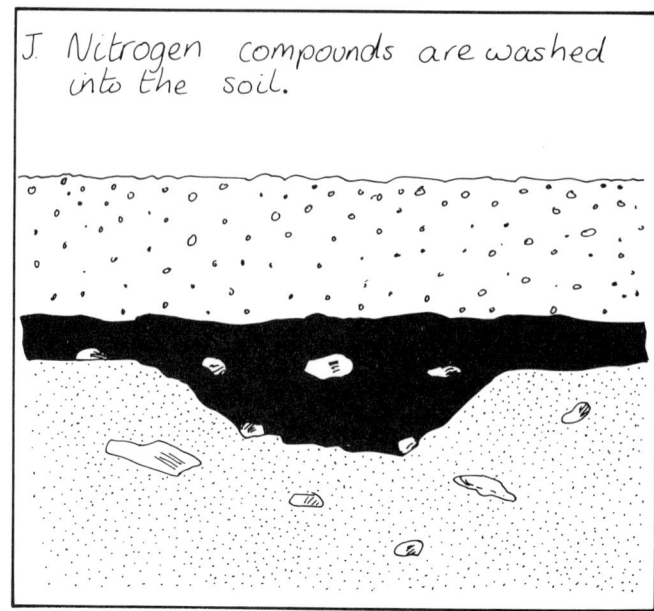

Food chains

A food chain shows that one living thing is eaten by another.
Food chains always start with plants and go towards animals.

For example: lettuce leaf ─▷ snail ─▷ thrush

- Cut out and arrange these pictures in 3 food chains.
- Check your ideas with your teacher.
- If you are correct paste them in your book, drawing arrows to connect them.

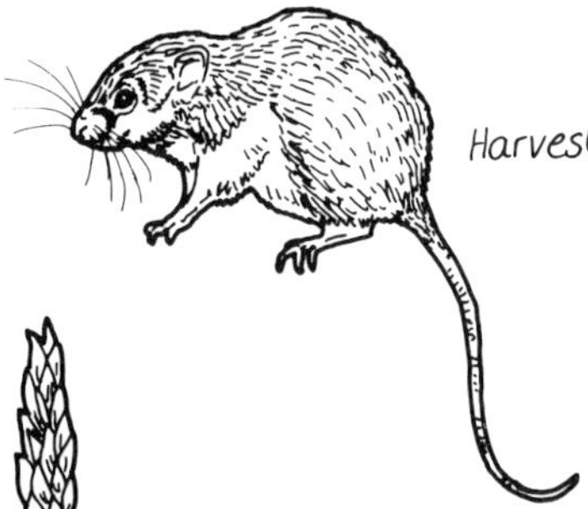

Harvest mouse

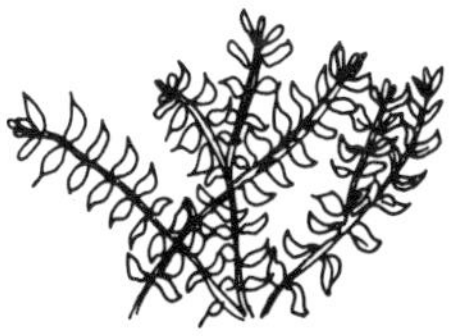

Pondweed

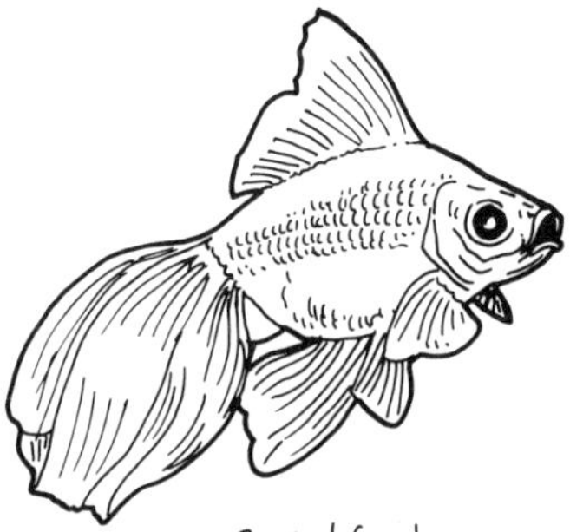

Goldfish

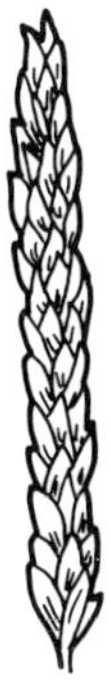

Wheat

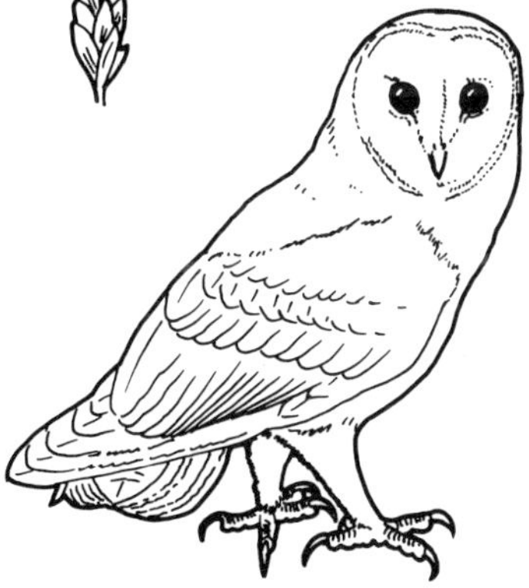

Grass

Barn owl

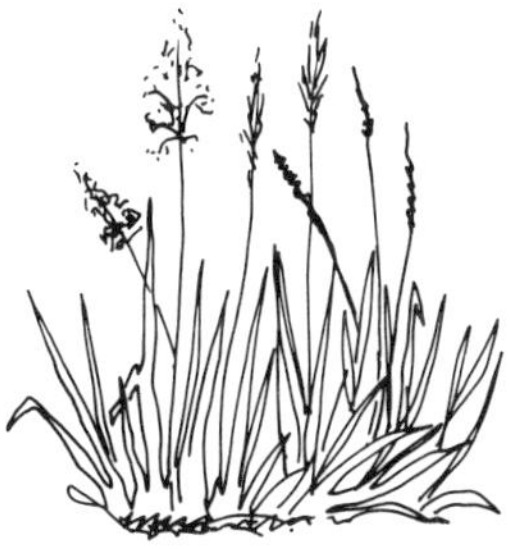

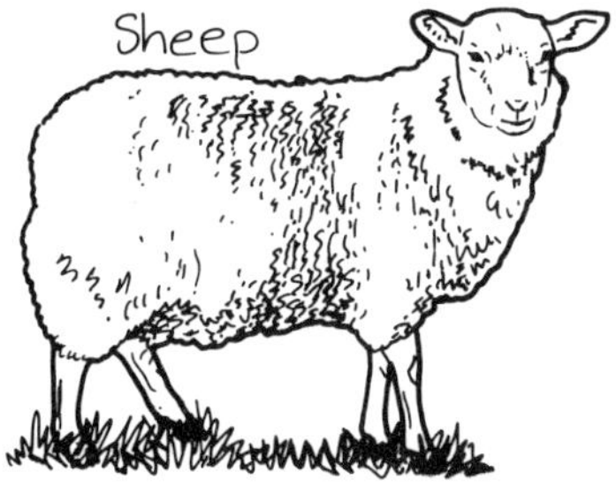

Sheep

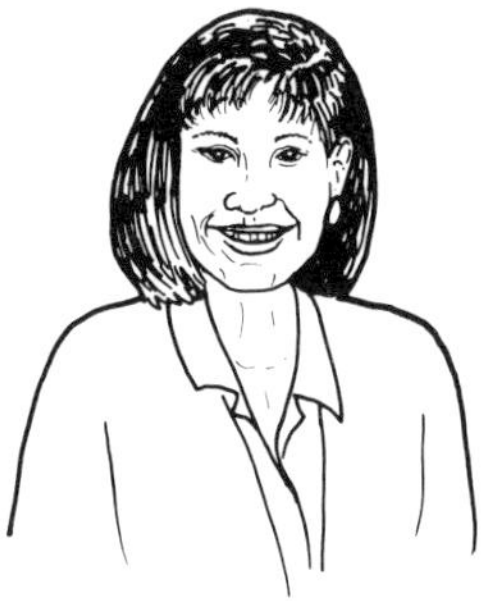

Person

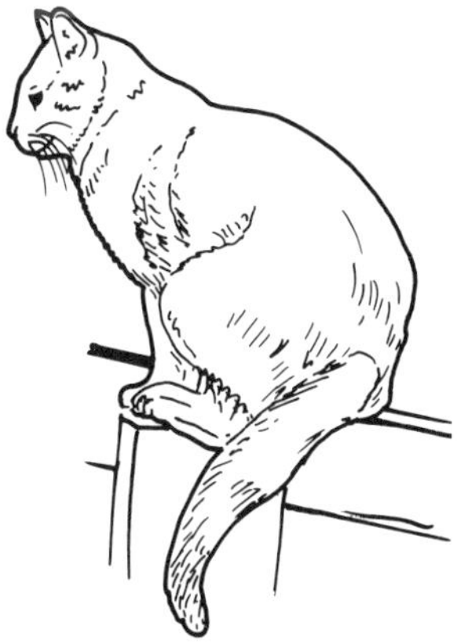

Cat

Our bodies - notes and suggestions

Skin and touch (Sc2: KS1, 2a)
How good is your sense of touch? You will need two large pins and a cork for each pair of pupils to test their skin sensitivity. Use the heads not the points of the pins. You could draw a diagram of the body and mark on different sensitivities.

Taking care of your skin (Sc2: KS1, 2a)
This is an introduction to clean skin, cleansing wounds and killing germs with antiseptics. No demonstration or observations of open wounds or blood are advised. The topic could lead into skin care and cosmetics.

Smoking can damage your health (Sc2: KS3, 2a)
A demonstration of a 'smoking machine', where smoke from a cigarette is drawn through a cotton wool filter by a vacuum pump, is a vivid demonstration of what enters the lungs. There are videos and wall charts available from the Health Councils to supplement this activity.

Taste (Sc2: KS1, 2b)
This blindfold activity for tasting can give anxiety to some pupils who do not like to have their eyes covered. It can be done with eyes open but without looking at what is being eaten. A peg on the nose often removes 'hints' of what the fruit is, smell and taste being closely linked. Use pieces of the same size e.g. cubes.

Reactions
This activity is easily done and could lead to a graph of results. Results sometimes show an improvement in a person's skill, then a slight decline due to tiredness and boredom. Link this activity to the need to be alert when driving. Let the pupils design a reaction experiment to test responses to sound.

Your eyes (Sc2: KS3, 5f)
If pupils wear glasses they can test with/without them on. The need for good eyesight in both eyes gives us an ability to see things in 3-D. Due to problems with their eyes, some pupils will have difficulty with 3-D perception and perspective, but everyone has difficulty with one eye closed.

Animal eyes (Sc2: KS3, 5f)
Collect pictures to produce a display illustrating differences in body form between prey and predatory animals.

Ears and hearing (Sc2: KS3, 2k, 2j)
This activity will reveal that the ears can help 3-D location and demonstrate that we often supplement our sight with hearing and vice-versa. Pupils with a hearing loss will not necessarily find this difficult or embarrassing but it will help them to understand how sounds reach us. You could discuss the purpose of ear shapes of both humans and animals.

All senses
This activity reinforces an understanding of how our senses detect information in the environment.

Fooling your senses
Students should be encouraged to make predictions before they measure the lines and then to discuss how the illusion has fooled them! A sound quiz can be a follow-up.

Mirror tricks! (Sc4, 3c)
This looks at how our co-ordination depends very much on our expectations of what will happen. It should also demonstrate a learning process. If the star shape is too difficult, use a triangle.

How good is your sense of touch? 1 and 2
Put a selection of objects with different textures inside the box. Take each activity separately or make a 3 activity circus with pupils rotating!

Energy foods (Sc2: 2c)
You will need a dilute solution of iodine in potassium iodine to do the experiment. A test for starch is that it gives a blue/black colour with iodine solution. Pictures of different foods from magazines will supplement this activity.

Foods for health (Sc2: 2e, 2q)
The discussion of 'junk' food leads pupils to understand what is meant by nutrients and balanced diets. Emphasise that some junk food is ok but not all the time.

Health farm (Sc2: 2q, 2r, 2s)
This activity encourages students to make inferences from graphical data. They will need help interpreting the graph. Phone your health centre, they have some good free literature.

Teeth (Sc2: KS2, 2a)
Many people are surprised to see their tooth patterns when indented on plasticine as compared with what they feel with their tongue in their mouth.

Skeletons and organs (Sc2: KS3, 2g)
These two activities will help pupils to learn about the structure of their bodies and understand the role of the skeleton in support. A model skeleton is a useful resource.

NATIONAL CURRICULUM INFORMATION

The activities address science in the National Curriculum and can be cross-referenced to sections of the Programme of Study and topics mentioned in the Attainment Target level descriptions (levels 1–4). Some activities refer to more than one section and some to other subject areas.

The activities give opportunities for addressing Attainment Target 1, Experimental and Investigative Science, in a safe way.

Skin and touch

Our Bodies
cork with matchsticks stuck into it.

- Work with a partner.
- Gently place the matchsticks on different parts of your partner's body.
- Let either 1 or 2 matchsticks touch the skin but make sure your partner cannot see the matchsticks.
- Can your partner feel 2 matchsticks or 1?
- Try each place **twice**, then write down if they were right or wrong.
- Then get your partner to test you.

Here are the results of my test:

Part of body	right	wrong
back of hand		
palm of hand		
front of arm		
back of arm		
neck (front and back)		
cheek		
forehead		
ankle		
knee		

The skin is the largest organ of your body.
It can sense touch and changes in temperature.

1. The skin covers your whole _____.

2. The part of the body that can sense touch best is the _____.

3. Why was it important to test each part of the body twice?
   _____.

4. The skin sends messages to the brain along _____.

Talk about how your skin helps you keep cool.

USEFUL WORDS
body
sweat
skin
hot
nerves
germs

© 1992 Folens Ltd. This page may be photocopied for classroom use only

Taking care of your skin

It hurts when you scrape or cut your knee because the skin's nerve endings get damaged.
The pain stops when the nerves begin to repair themselves.

1. Why do you need to clean the cut and put a cream on it?
   _____
   _____

2. Here are the letters of a word that means 'germ killer': **ASPICNEITT**

   The word is _____.

3. List 3 ways that germs can get into our body.

   Way 1 _____

   Way 2 _____

   Way 3 _____

4. You can stop germs getting into your body by
   _____
   _____
   _____
   _____

Talk about what you should do if you get an infection caused by a germ, and what doctors do to help.

Smoking can damage your health

1. People who smoke cannot smell or taste as well as others. This might be because the smoke kills some _____.

2. The tar from smoking can also cause some terrible diseases like lung _____ and _____ disease.

USEFUL WORDS
nerves
heart
cancer

• Design a sign that could be put up in your school or in a public place to stop people smoking or even not to start smoking.

Here is the design for my sign:

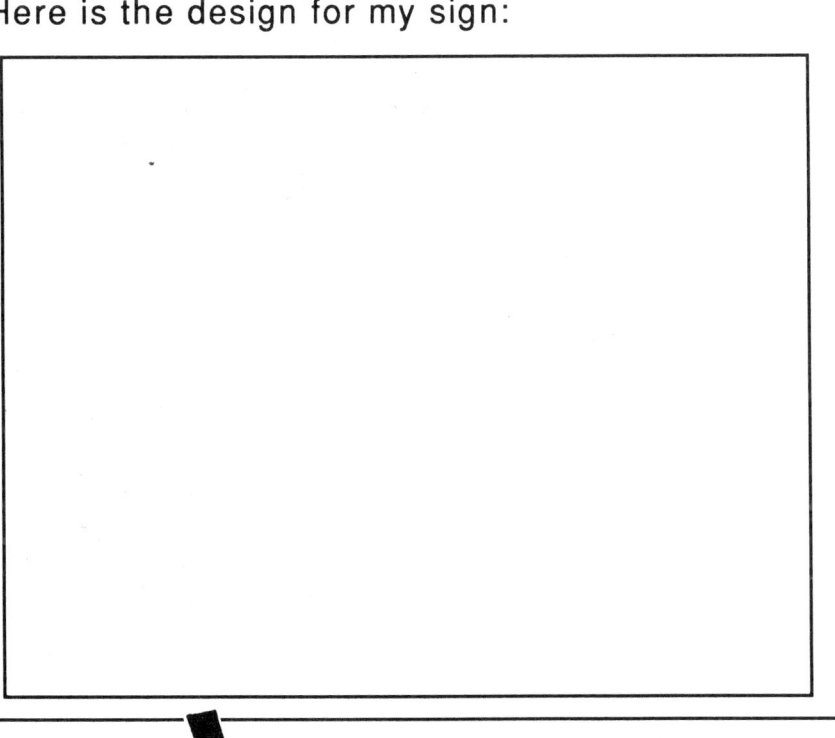

A lot of money is spent on treating people with smoking related diseases.
Many people believe that smoking should be banned in public places and places of work. What do you think? Talk about these issues. Find out what proportion of the class agree with smoking.

© 1992 Folens Ltd. This page may be photocopied for classroom use only Page 23

Our Bodies

Taste

selection of fruit cut into pieces

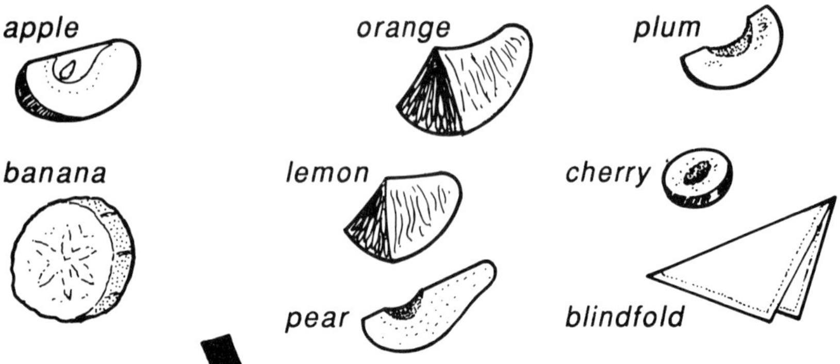

apple  orange  plum

banana  lemon  cherry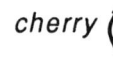

pear 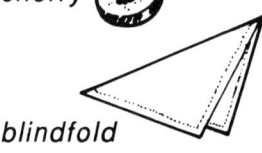 blindfold

You need

Investigate

- Blindfold your partner.
- Feed him/her small pieces of fruit.
- Get your partner to say the name of the fruits they tasted.
- Write down which ones they got right and then get them to test you.

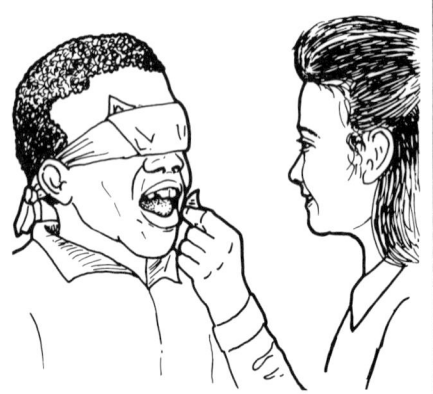

Fill in the results.
A tick shows that we got the taste right.
A cross shows that we got the taste wrong.

Name of fruit	My results	My partner's results

How important is it to see the fruit to be able to name it? _____

What I found

Talk about what will happen if you hold your nose as well as being blindfolded during this experiment.

Reactions

Our Bodies
ruler

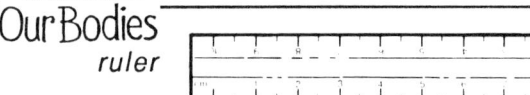

 You need

 Investigate

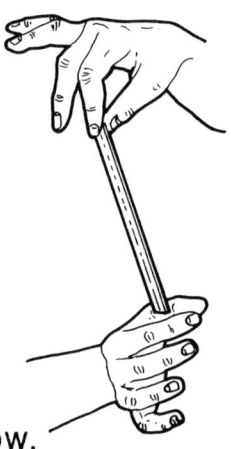

- Work with a partner.
- Get your partner to hold the ruler level with your open finger and thumb then let go.
- Close to grip the ruler as quickly as you can.
- Measure how many centimetres are below your fingers.
- Get your partner to test you three times, then test your partner.
- Fill in your results on the chart below.

Fast reactions mean that your body can sense something happening and respond to it very quickly.

Results:

Attempt	Reading on ruler (cm.)	
	Me	My partner
1		
2		
3		

 What I found

1. Did your reactions get quicker? _____

2. Who had the faster reactions?

_____

Find out if the reaction with your other hand is as fast as the hand you tested.

3. What other way can you think of to measure the speed of your reactions?

_____

Talk about why it is important for you to have fast reactions.

Our Bodies

Your eyes

Your eyes are very important for you to react to changes in your surroundings.

- Work with a partner.
- Look into your partner's eyes.
- Draw the shapes and colours you can see.

- Get your partner to close his/her eyes and count to 20 then open their eyes.
- Look again at the centre part of each eye.
- Ask them to look towards the window.
- Did you notice any changes in the eyes?

_____

- Look at a diagram of the eye.
  What parts of the eye changed during your experiment?

_____

Being able to use both eyes to look at an object is called binocular vision. Devise a test to compare vision between one and two eyes. Talk about what differences you noticed.

© 1992 Folens Ltd.   This page may be photocopied for classroom use only

Animal eyes

Our Bodies

- Name these animals which have eyes on each side of their head.

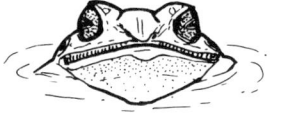

- Name 3 animals, like us, which have eyes pointing towards the front.

Animals with eyes pointing to the front

- Name an animal which has eyes on the top of its head.

_____

Talk about why each animal depends on the position of its eyes to find food and escape their enemies.

Ears and hearing

blindfold

access to an open space

- Blindfold one person and stand them inside a ring of children.
- One of the people in the ring claps their hands.
- The blindfolded person points to where he/she thinks the sound was made, but without moving their feet.
- Each person in the ring makes their sound several times during the experiment.
- One of the people in the ring fills in a 'listening map', like the one shown.
- Each tick shows when he/she pointed correctly to where a sound was made.

✓ = Right
✗ = Wrong
■ = Clap

1. What does this experiment tell you about your hearing?
   _____

2. What does this experiment tell you about the hearing of other people?
   _____

3. If you cover your left ear and try the test again, how would you expect the results to be different?
   _____

Talk about how well you can tell where the sound is coming from.

© 1992 Folens Ltd.   This page may be photocopied for classroom use only

Our Bodies

All senses

- Imagine that 5 people in the table have lost one sense. Put a ✗ if the person is unable to do the task. Put a ✔ if they can do the task.

	No taste	No hearing	No sight	No smell	No feeling in hands
Is the watch ticking?					
Does the sweet have a nice taste?					
Is the flower red or white?					
Is the cup hot or cold?					
Is the picture colourful?					
Are you wearing perfume?					

If you know anyone who has lost the use of one or more of their senses, ask them what tasks they find difficult.
Talk about how they cope with them.

© 1992 Folens Ltd. This page may be photocopied for classroom use only

Fooling your senses

1. Look at this drawing. Does it show an old woman or a young lady?
   _____

2. Are these two lines parallel? _____
   Check your guess with a ruler.

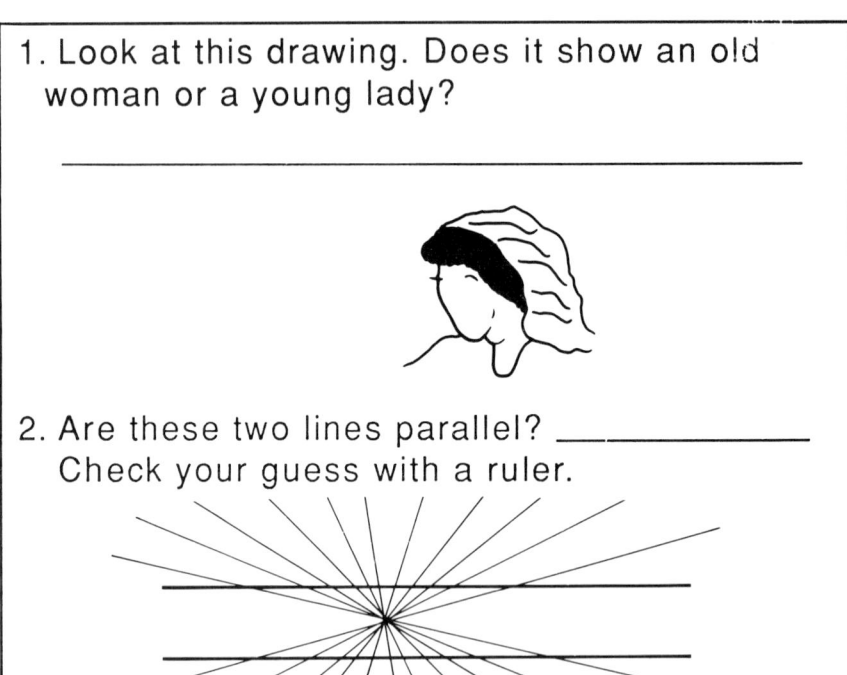

3. Which line is the longest? A, B or C? _____
   Check your guess with a ruler.

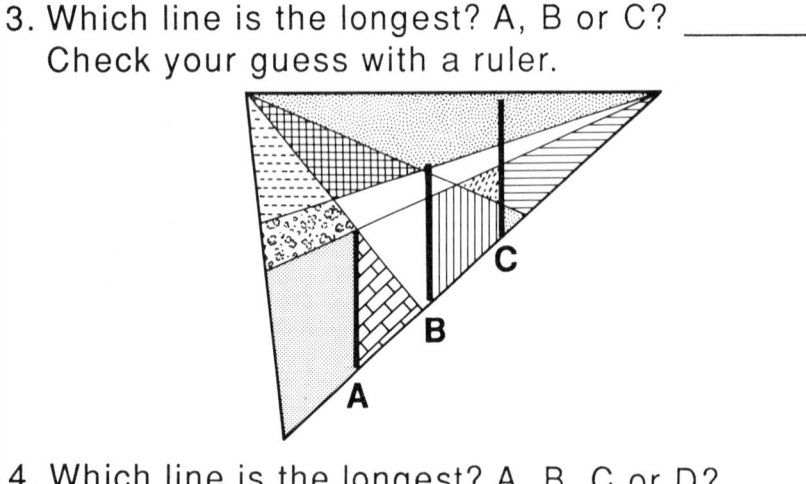

4. Which line is the longest? A, B, C or D? _____
   Check your guess with a ruler.

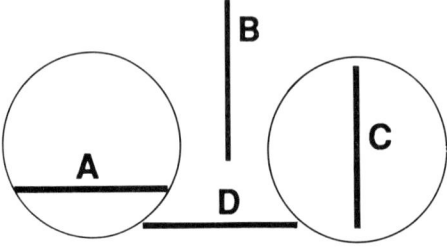

Talk about which diagrams on this page fooled your senses. Draw another diagram that could fool someone else's eyes.

Mirror tricks!

Our Bodies

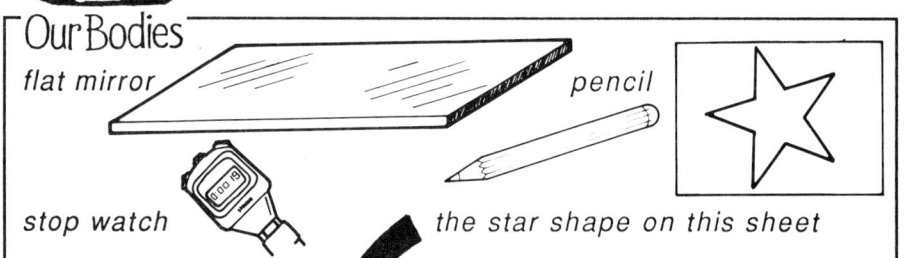

flat mirror   pencil   the star shape on this sheet

stop watch

You need

Investigate

- Put your star shape next to a mirror so that you can see the shape of the star in the mirror (see diagram).
- By looking in the mirror **only**, use a pencil to trace around the star.
- Time how long it took to go round the star.
- Try the test 3 times.

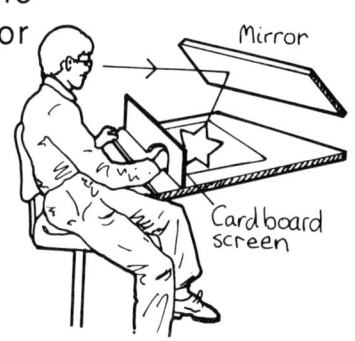

Here is my table of results:

Attempt	Time to trace star
1	
2	
3	

1. I think it is easy/hard to trace around the star because

   _____

2. Do your results show that you learned how to trace around the star?

   _____

What I found

Talk about what this says about how you learn.

© 1992 Folens Ltd.   This page may be photocopied for classroom use only

How good is your sense of touch? 1

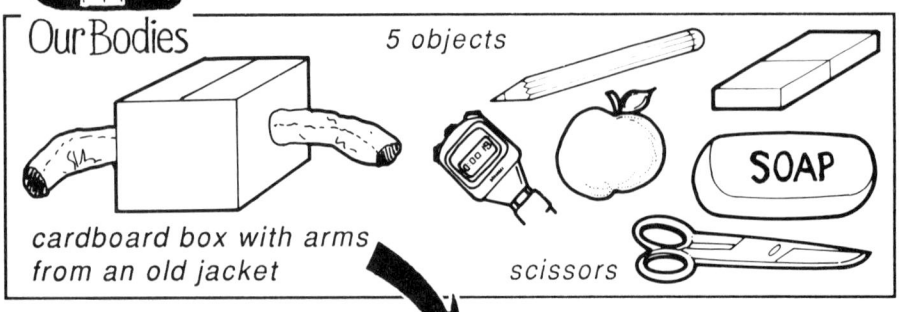

Our Bodies

5 objects

cardboard box with arms from an old jacket

scissors

You need

Investigate

- Place inside the covered cardboard box a number of objects. Don't show anyone.
- Get your friend to feel them and try and say what they are.
- At the end of the experiment open the box to check their answers.
- Put a tick or cross in the table showing your results.
- Now get your friend to do the same to you but with different objects.

List of objects in the box	tick or cross	
	partner's results	my results

1. Which objects were the most difficult to name? _____

And now...

Talk about why some objects are easier to identify.

How good is your sense of touch? 2

Our Bodies

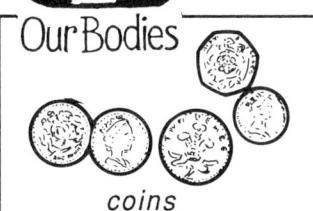
coins

paper

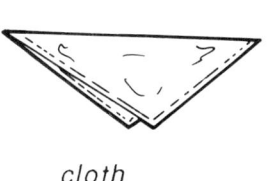
cloth

You need

Investigate

- Place a few coins in front of your partner.
- With his/her eyes closed, see if they can sort out which coins are which.
- Get them to try and feel which is the heads and which the tails side.
- Now get your partner to test you.

How does a blind person work out which coin is which?

_____

- Place a piece of paper on a soft surface, such as a cloth.
- Draw either a shape or a letter of the alphabet.
- Don't show your partner.
- See if they can feel with their eyes closed the dent on the paper and work out what you have drawn.
- How big does the shape have to be for them to work it out?

_____

- Now get your partner to try this test on you.

And now...

Talk about how you can tell what something is without seeing it.

Find out about the Braille language, its patterns and how it was invented.

© 1992 Folens Ltd.   This page may be photocopied for classroom use only   Page 33

Energy foods

Cars need fuel to go, we need food fuel to live. Foods containing substances called carbohydrates give our body most of the energy it needs.

- Find out if these foods in the list below contain the carbohydrate called starch in them.
- Put a drop of iodine solution on a small amount of each food.
- If it goes dark blue or black tick the chart to show there is starch in the food.

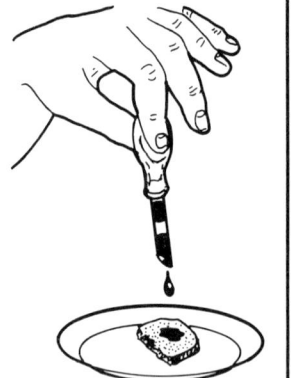

Fill in this table with your results:

Food	tick or cross
white bread	
brown bread	
flour	
lettuce	
piece of apple	
piece of potato	
potato crisp	
sugar	
salt/cheese or milk	

List the foods that contain starch:

_____

_____

_____

Talk about the other things you must have in your diet.

© 1992 Folens Ltd.   This page may be photocopied for classroom use only

Foods for health

Food for healthy living must have a good mixture of chemicals we call nutrients. Foods that do not have many nutrients are called 'junk' food.

Healthy foods include a balanced mixture of carbohydrates, proteins, vitamins, minerals, fats and water. Junk food contains only small amounts of this balanced mixture.

- List the following as 'Junk food' or 'Good food'.

Name of food	junk/good
bread	
crisps	
sweets	
meat	
vegetables	
milk	
fruit	
fish	
lemonade	

- Put together a balanced set of healthy meals for one day. Don't over eat!

Breakfast

Lunch

Tea or Supper

x4

Health farm

My older sister went on holiday to a health farm for a week with her boyfriend. Her name is Ann and his name is Bodi.

	Ann	Bodi
Height	150cm	180cm
Weight at the start	60kg	100kg
Weight after one week	50kg	80kg
Sports	walking and jogging	snooker and darts

• Look at this graph supplied by the Health Centre.

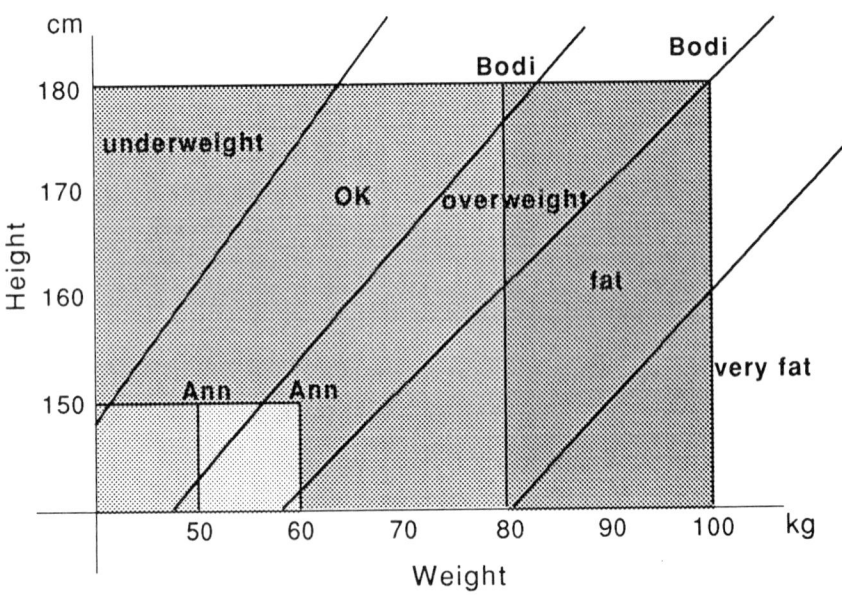

Look at Ann and Bodi's weight at the start and at the end of the week.
What advice would you give to Ann and Bodi?

_____

_____

Talk about what Ann and Bodi did during the week to lose the weight.

Our Bodies

Teeth

When a new baby is born it already has teeth hidden under its gums ready to grow through later.
They are called 'milk' teeth or baby teeth and there are usually 20 of them. When you are grown up you should have 32 teeth.

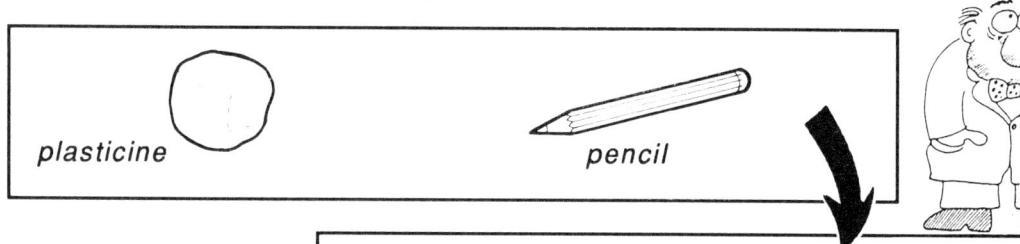

You need:

plasticine   pencil

- When do a baby's teeth usually begin to grow through their gums? (Ask a mother.)

_____

- Bite on a piece of plasticine to see what your tooth pattern looks like.
- Draw it.

Investigate

Draw a poster to give your friends some hints on taking care of their teeth.

Talk about how to keep healthy teeth.

© 1992 Folens Ltd.   This page may be photocopied for classroom use only

Skeletons and organs

Skeletons

- Join up the words to the various bones of the body.

  fingers
  skull
  jaw
  ribs
  vertebrae
  pelvis
  radius
  ulna
  femur
  tibia
  toes

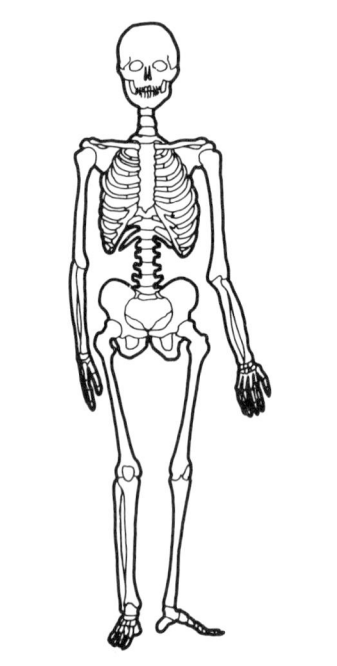

Organs

- Join up the words to the various organs of the body.

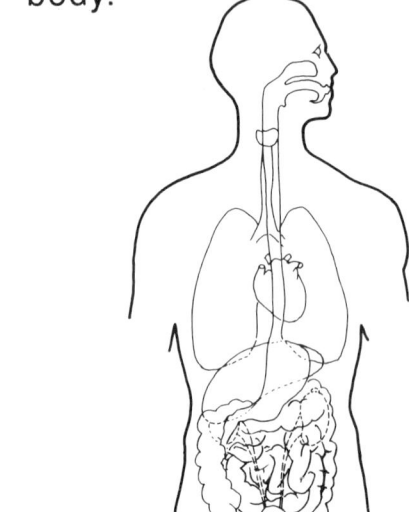

  heart
  liver
  lungs
  kidney
  intestine

  reproductive-organs

Talk about why the different parts of your body are where they are.

© 1992 Folens Ltd.   This page may be photocopied for classroom use only

Our world - notes and suggestions

The world
This activity overlaps with geography and helps in the planning of cross-curricular activities. Some pupils have little understanding of distance or the shape of the continents. You will need some maps.

Weather
This helps pupils to understand how external factors, such as weather, affect our lives. Weather rhymes can also be made up and their accuracy tested.

Weather chart
This activity requires a longer time to complete but will promote continuity.

Rain measuring
This is both an activity for pupils to do and also for interpretation of results. You need clear plastic drink bottles.

Make an air thermometer (KS3: Sc3, 2a, 2c, 2d, 2e)
A 'class-made' thermometer can be made to show the principle that temperature changes are measured by something expanding and contracting. A commercial thermometer can be used for prolonged temperature measurements.

Waste monitor
This activity helps pupils to appreciate the amount of waste that is disposed of. You could do a scaling up exercise to see how much is wasted by a class in a month, year, etc.

Natural resources
The pupils will need a bit of help to show the difference between natural and manufactured objects.

Rocks (Sc3, 2f)
You will need samples of soil, sand and gravel, a sloping tray, a watering can, plaster of paris and water. The mould can be made of stiff card or wood. Fair testing should be done on the plaster blocks. Suggest mixtures of plaster of paris and water in different proportions.

Space (Sc4: KS3, 4a, 4b, 4c, 4d)
Pupils have difficulty in visualising the motion of the heavenly bodies but it is a set of systems that are around us. Models can help as will the story of Galileo and other astronomers. Pupils could produce a display of pictures of the moon, planets, space ships etc. which can add reality, as can looking at the moon with binoculars but NOT THE SUN. Some excellent videos are available e.g., Scientific Eye series.

NATIONAL CURRICULUM INFORMATION

The activities address science in the National Curriculum and can be cross-referenced to sections of the Programme of Study and topics mentioned in the Attainment Target level descriptions (levels 1–4). Some activities refer to more than one section and some to other subject areas.

The activities give opportunities for addressing Attainment Target 1, Experimental and Investigative Science, in a safe way.

© 1992 Folens Ltd.

The world

- Look at the map of the world. Colour in Britain.

1. Britain is surrounded by _____.

2. The map shows six of the seven c_____. Their names are:

   A: _____.

   B: _____.

   C: _____.

   D: _____.

   E: _____.

   F: _____.

3. Look at a model of the Earth or an atlas and find the name of the continent covering the South Pole.

   The continent is called _____.

4. The ice cap covering the North Pole is called the _____

5. Use an atlas to see where the equator runs. Draw a line across your map to show the equator.

USEFUL WORDS
continents
sea
arctic
antarctica

Weather

The lives of most living things are affected by the type of weather where they live. Different living things respond to the weather in different ways.

- How did the weather affect you today?
  Did you wear a coat?
  _____

  Why?
  _____
  _____

- What is your favourite weather? _____

- Does everyone in your class enjoy the same type of weather?
  _____

  Draw a chart of people's favourite weather.

1. Look out of the window. Describe in words or draw a picture of the type of clouds and the weather you can see.
   _____
   _____
   _____
   _____
   _____
   _____
   _____

2. How can you predict weather?
   _____
   _____

Weather chart

- Use a line to join up the symbols with the correct weather words. The first one has been done for you.

SUNNY   RAIN   CLOUDY   SUNNY SPELLS   LIGHTNING   SNOW

- Keep your own Weather Chart for 1 week. Use the symbols above and make up any others you need.

- Forecast the weather. Fill in these spaces.

The weather today is _____

My forecast for tomorrow is _____

Actual weather _____

Test your forecast. How close were you?

- What information do you need to make an accurate weather forecast?

USEFUL WORDS
sunny
spells
sunny
rain
thunder
snow
cloudy

Talk about why some believe a dance can make it rain.

© 1992 Folens Ltd.   This page may be photocopied for classroom use only   Page 42

Rain measuring

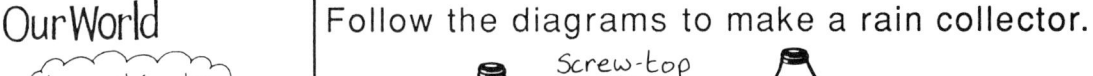

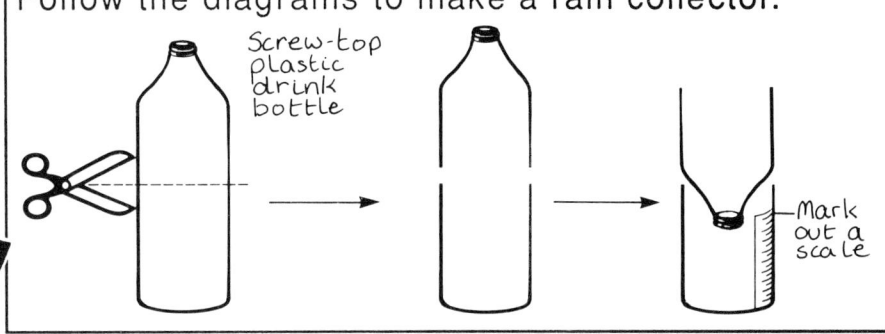

Follow the diagrams to make a rain collector.

Screw-top plastic drink bottle

Mark out a scale

- Place your rain collector in a good place - not too close to buildings or under trees.
- Sink the bottom of the bottle in the soil to stop it falling over.
- Measure the rainfall over a few weeks.

Date	Rain	Measurement

- Plot a bar graph of your results.

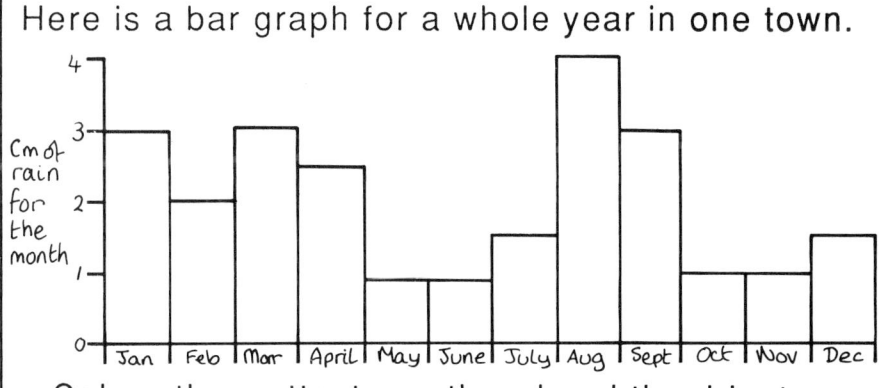

Here is a bar graph for a whole year in one town.

- Colour the wettest month red and the driest months blue.
- How much rain fell during the whole year? _____ cm.

Talk about how the amount of rain affects different countries.

Make an air thermometer

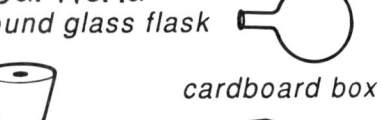

Our World
- round glass flask
- long glass tube
- cardboard box
- coloured water
- bung
- ruler

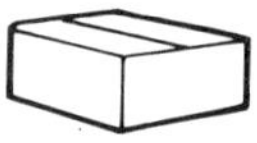

Investigate

- Fit a long glass tube and cork into the flask.
- Warm the flask with your hands for a few minutes.
- Dip the end of the tube under the surface of the coloured water.
- Fit the neck of the flask into the slot of a cut cardboard box.
- Fix a ruler marked in centimetres behind the tube of water.
- From time to time, measure how much the level of water in the long tube goes up and down as the temperature of the air in the room changes.

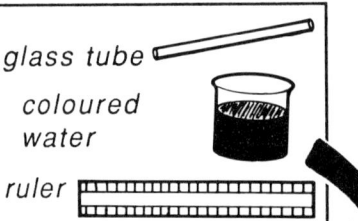

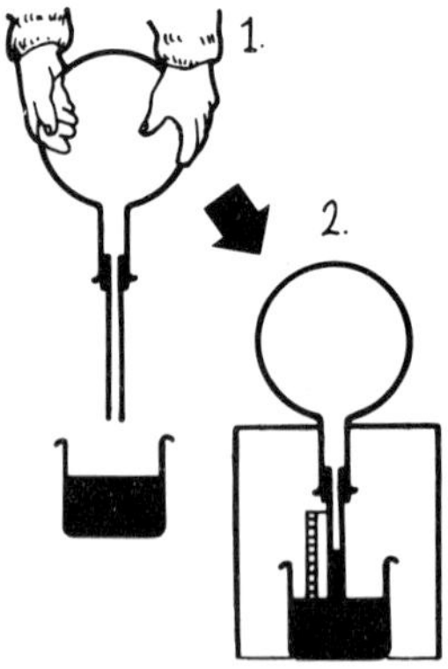

USEFUL WORDS
thermometer
degrees

What I found

1. Fill in this table of results.

Time of day	Height of liquid

2. Draw a graph to show your results.

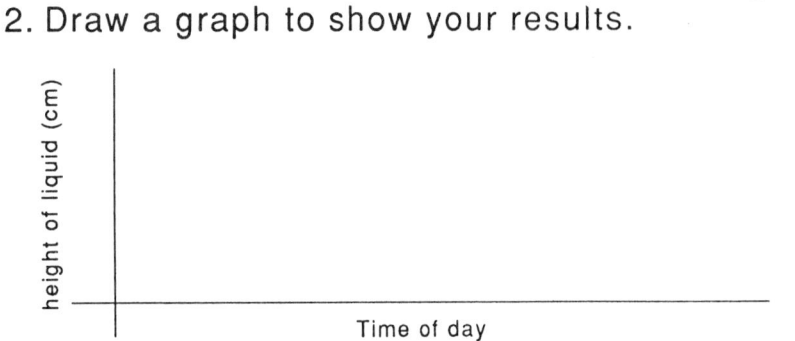

height of liquid (cm) vs Time of day

Talk about why the graph has the shape that it does.
A more accurate way of measuring temperature is by using a mercury thermometer. Temperature is measured in degrees Celsius (0°C).

Waste monitor

Our environment is threatened by waste of various sorts. If this waste is not put in the correct place it causes pollution.

- List the sorts of waste you have thrown away today.

_____

_____

- Look around your school. What waste can you find? Where did you find it?

Name of waste	Where I found it

- What could the paper be used for if it was all collected?

_____

_____

Design a poster to encourage people to save waste paper.

Talk about how other people waste materials that can be re-used.

Natural resources

A natural resource is something that is found **free** in nature which people can use.

- Put a tick to show which of these items are natural or manufactured.

Item	natural	manufactured
metals		
cars		
bicycles		
wood		
air		
water		
fish		
TV		
clothes		
fruit		
rocks		
books		
oil		
coal		

Things made from natural resources can often be recycled.
I think recycling means _____
_____
_____

Talk about why a bottle bank is important in recycling glass.

Design a poster to encourage people to recycle waste.

Rocks

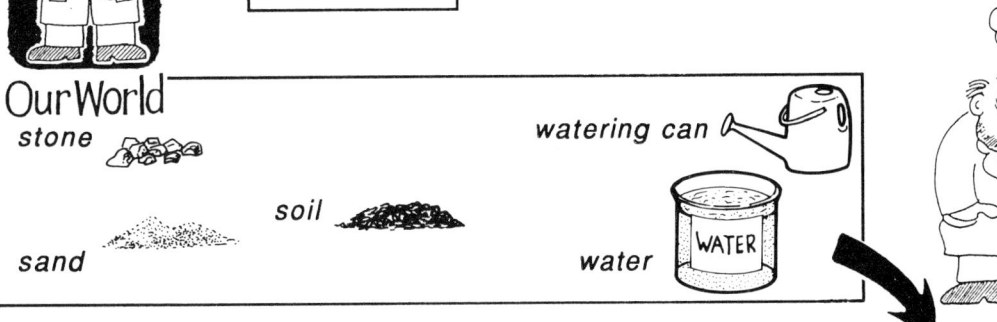

Our World
- stone
- sand
- soil
- watering can
- water

You need

And now...

- Make a set of mixtures containing sand, soil and stone. They should all weigh the same amount.
- Put each mixture on top of the slope.
- Water each pile from a watering can.
- Write down or draw a line to show where the sand, soil and stones end up.

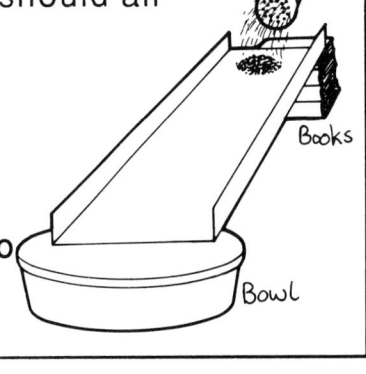

Books
Bowl

What I found

1. What does this tell you about the things in soil?

   _____
   _____
   _____

2. What does this tell you about how rivers and mountain streams change the shape of the land?

   _____
   _____
   _____

A sand and gravel company wants a big poster to show how sand is made from rocks.
Can you produce one for them?
Talk about how such companies affect our environment.

Space

Our World

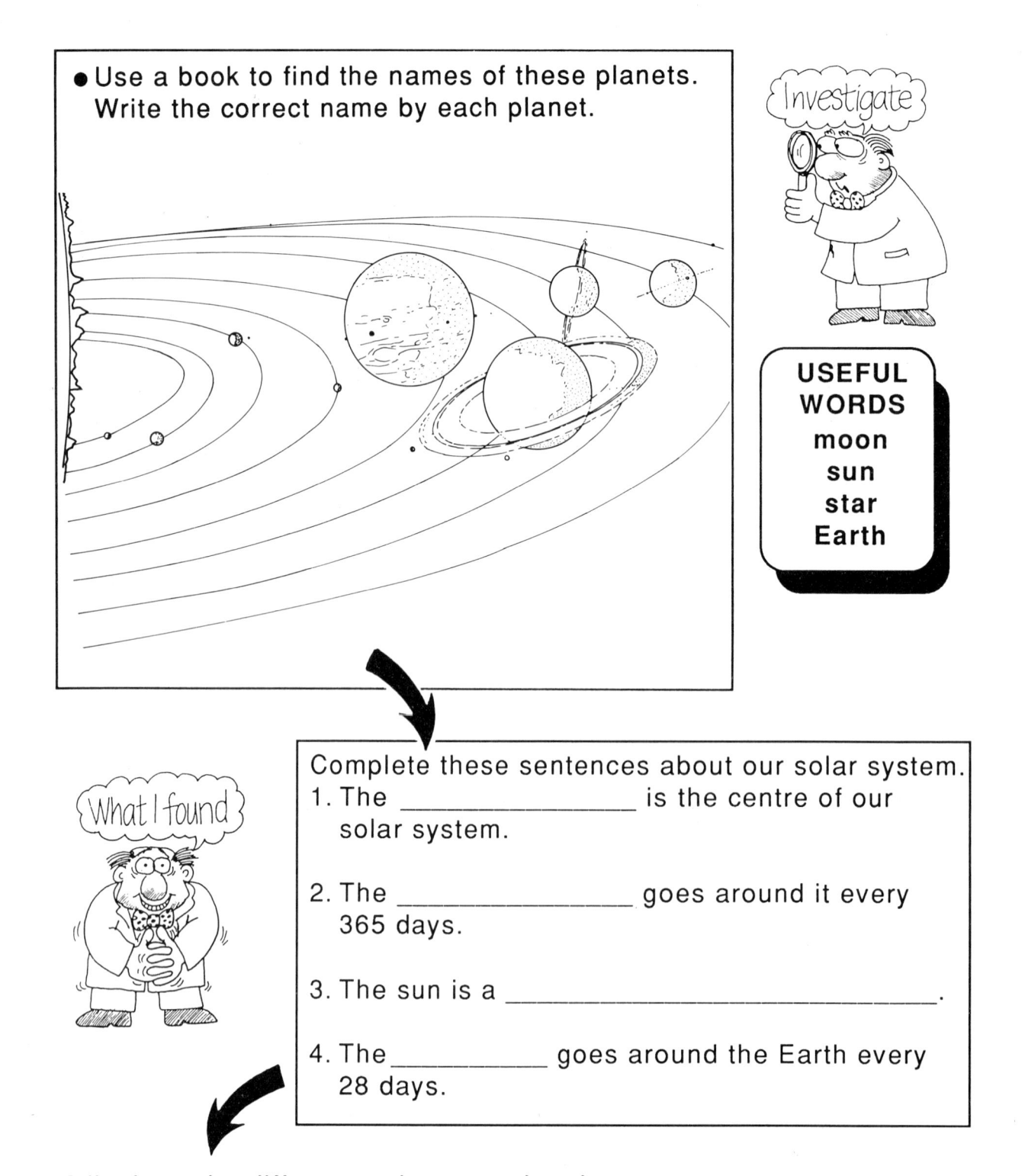

The Earth is one of the planets in the solar system.

Investigate

- Use a book to find the names of these planets. Write the correct name by each planet.

USEFUL WORDS
moon
sun
star
Earth

What I found

Complete these sentences about our solar system.

1. The _____ is the centre of our solar system.

2. The _____ goes around it every 365 days.

3. The sun is a _____.

4. The _____ goes around the Earth every 28 days.

Talk about the differences between the planets, are they all the same size? Do they look alike?

© 1992 Folens Ltd.   This page may be photocopied for classroom use only